Operation Crescent Moon

**Underground
Christians Reaching
Muslims in the Land
of Mohammed**

GEORGE JOHN

PIONEER BOOK COMPANY
CANEY KANSAS

Bible quotations are taken from the *New International Version*, © 1973, 1978, 1984 by International Bible Society, published by Zondervan Publishing House, Grand Rapids, Michigan.

Operation Crescent Moon

© 1994 by Pioneer Book Company

Published by
Pioneer Book Company
P.O. Box 284, Caney, KS 67333

Library of Congress Cataloging-in-Publication Data
John, George M.
    Operation Crescent Moon : underground Christians reaching Muslims in the land of Mohammed / George John. — 1st ed.
        p.   cm.
    Translated from Malayalam.
    ISBN 0-88264-307-X : $5.00
    1. Missions to Muslims—Arabian Peninsula. 2. John, George M. 3. Missionaries—Arabian Peninsula—Biography. 4. Missionaries—India—Biography. 5. Persecution—Arabian Peninsula—History—20th century. I. Title.
BV2625.J59   1994
266'.00953—dc20   94-2150
                                                          CIP

Printed in the United States of America.

Names of individuals in this book have been changed to protect their identity.

Dedication

To Raymond Lully—the first Christian missionary to the Muslims. He left a comfortable position as professor at Oxford and spent most of his life suffering for the gospel.

When shipwrecked near Pisa after many years of missionary labor, though nearly seventy, his ardor was unabated.

"Once," he wrote, "I was fairly rich; once I had a wife and children; once I tasted freely of the pleasures of this life. But all these things I gladly resigned that I might spread abroad a knowledge of the truth.

"I studied Arabic and several times went forth to preach the gospel to the Saracens. I have been in prisons; I have been scourged; for years I have striven to persuade the princes of Christendom to befriend the common cause of converting the Mohammedans. Now, though old and poor, I do not despair; I am ready, if it be God's will, to persevere unto death."

And he died so, being stoned to death in Bugia, Africa, in 1314 after gathering a little flock of converts.

Contents

Prologue

Y̶ou must excuse me, but I have to blindfold you."

"Why?" Brother James, a Christian visitor from India, tightly gripped the armrest of his chair as his hosts slid the kerchief over his eyes and fastened it behind his head. "Don't you trust me?"

"We can't take any chances," came the calm reply as the driver of the large American car sped away from the airport.

On a secret mission, it was James' first venture into this Arab country. He found it impossible to maintain any sense of direction as the car turned this way and that around countless corners for the next hour. Sitting low on the back seat to avoid attracting attention, he had time to think. *Are these men who they say they are? They knew I was arriving from Ethiopia and met me as scheduled. This is Saudi Arabia, not a Communist country, so why the blindfold? Don't they know I'm a committed Christian?*

Brother James' thoughts played cat-and-mouse with his feelings as he tried to reassure himself that all was well. Unable to shake his uneasiness, he put his head back. *Maybe it's be-*

cause I'm tired. He opened his eyes a crack, but no light penetrated his blindfold. He decided to relax and concentrate on sound. Judging from the traffic noises and start-and-stop driving, they were still in the city. *A big city*, he mused, trying to calculate time, speed, and distance. But his thoughts were unfocused. *Too many variables. Besides, I am tired.*

Suddenly, the car jerked to a stop, and this time the driver cut the engine. Someone opened the door and helped James out, then two men guided him into a building where the blindfold was removed. He blinked, relieved to be in a lovely home rather than—he thought sheepishly—a police station.

The large, carpeted, beautifully furnished living room surprised him. He could have been in a modern American home. On the side table was a birthday cake, complete with candles. About a dozen men in Arab dress eyed him expectantly, but before they could exchange amenities his host escorted him to a clothes closet at the far side of the room. "Get inside. Quickly," he urged.

Having little choice in the matter, James complied. He stood crammed into a corner for about fifteen minutes as the group talked excitedly among themselves in a tongue foreign to him. Was it joy—or fear? He shifted, reassuring himself that he was a privileged guest in an underground church in a Muslim land.

Finally, the door opened, and he stepped out, taking a deep breath.

His host, who spoke English and acted as a translator, smiled. "Because you are a stranger, it was necessary to hide you in case it was the police who were at the door. You will know where to go immediately if someone knocks," he warned. Then he introduced Brother James to the group of thirteen men. No names were mentioned, for reasons James could understand.

Though they represented one of seven underground churches in this Muslim stronghold, the occasion was ostensibly a birthday party. Underground Christians in repressive countries worldwide celebrate many a "birthday" to camouflage their activities and mislead unexpected visitors.

"As for the blindfold," the host explained, "it was necessary in case you were arrested and taken to the police station. In our country they have ways to make you talk. There are specialized drugs…" His voice trailed off. "A person tells everything he knows. We want to protect you— and ourselves. You should know that we don't usually associate with foreigners. We're afraid of betrayal.

"But come!" He smiled again and waved to the group. "Let's sing!"

The Christian from India joined his voice with fellow Christians in a Muslim country. He relaxed, breathing deeply. Music is indeed the language of the soul. His voice rose and fell in a familiar melody—then froze.

One of his Arab Christian brothers had no hands. He scanned the room. About half the Christians there were amputees. He remembered with a shudder that Muslims cut off the hand of anyone who converts to Christianity—an act of violence that deters all but those who are wholly committed to Jesus Christ.

The barbaric penalty—usually meted out to thieves—is implemented on Friday, the Muslim holy day. James thought of the irony: Friday is sacred to Christians as the day on which their Lord was crucified.

Regaining his composure, he joined in on the last hymn. Finally it was time for him to preach. Drawing on a lifetime of Christian experience, he fervently expounded the gospel, pointing to Christ as our all-sufficient Savior. It was a message of hope and courage undergirded with compassion. He had seen suffering before —had experienced it, in fact—but the memory of shortened arms clapping at the wrist would remain with him for the rest of his life.

He preached for an hour, including the translation, then joined in the refreshments. The bond of Christian fellowship was secure. No longer did Indian doubt Arab or Arab doubt Indian. In Christ all are one.

Two hours passed all too soon, and it was time to leave for the airport. Brother James embraced his newfound brethren, then smiled as the blindfold once again plunged him into darkness. He understood, hands quietly folded in his lap...

The Arabian Peninsula, so much in the news since the Gulf War, is a vast desert area extending some 1,500 miles from Jordan and Iraq on the north to the Arabian Sea to the south, and stretching 1,200 miles east to west at its widest point between the Red Sea and the Persian Gulf. The virtually rainless wasteland supports few plants and animals. With temperatures ranging as high as 130°F in the interior, it is inhospitable to man, though the Bedouin manage to survive as they search for water and pasture.

Most of the population is concentrated in seaports, where modern cities have sprung up like architects' dreams in the wake of enviable oil revenues. Arabia's claim to fame and fortune lies in its vast oil fields, discovered in the aftermath of World War II, giving the area an importance far beyond mere geography. Among the nations in the Middle East, Saudi Arabia has by far the largest territorial claim on this land mass.

For the most part, today's Arabs belong to the Muslim faith—Islam. Their religion has been the principal unifying element since the influence of Mohammed in the seventh century spread like a summer flood into the area we now broadly designate as the Middle East.

Originating in Palestine, Arabia's northern neighbor, Christianity had taken root principally in Asia Minor (today's Turkey) and Europe (notably Greece and Rome) through the efforts of the apostle Paul. As the center of Christianity turned westward over the centuries from Jerusalem to Constantinople to Rome, an accompanying shift in power and authority occurred. What Jesus had intended and Paul had preached —the priesthood of all believers—separated out like milk and cream into hierarchy and laity, them and us. Theology, of course, followed suit. The Scriptures themselves were restricted to a priesthood that claimed sole authority to interpret the mind of God.

By the beginning of the seventh century, as the Roman Catholic Church was consolidating its structures under Pope Gregory I, Mohammed—whose name in Arabic means "praised"— was having his own spiritual journey, which eventually led him to found Islam. Born in Mecca, he had visions that formed the basis of the Koran, perhaps the world's most influential book after the Bible.

One of the major reasons for the success of Islam in formerly Christian North Africa is the petty doctrinal squabbling of Christian leaders who had lost their evangelistic zeal. Today Arab/ Muslim influence dominates the Middle East. Although Jesus Christ is considered a worthy prophet along with Abraham, Moses, and of course Mohammed, Christians as a class are hated or at best tolerated. With the penalties so severe for converting to Christianity, it is little wonder that few Christians survive or their numbers increase slowly in the Arab Gulf countries or the nations of Iraq and Iran.

How, then, is it possible to get a toehold in this "crossroads of the East," where the flow of black gold dominates life, and the blessings of the "oil" of the Spirit are not even considered?

Oil itself is the answer. Labor needs are intense to construct and man the rigs, and third-world countries such as the Philippines and India, among others, have supplied a ready pool of cheap labor. Among these workers are many Christians.

Since as foreigners they can lose their jobs at any moment, they tend to be serious about their religion. Insecurity leads them to depend on the mercies of God rather than the whims of government. This kind of commitment invests them with a special fervor for sharing their faith in Christ and forming small groups. In addition, they are not so apt to be seen as imposing Western culture and religion, as are some Americans.

As for the Arabs themselves, many of their young people are sent to the United States to study—some at the invitation of American Christians working in Saudi Arabia. In American universities they meet Christians, and many are converted when they learn the truth about Jesus for the first time. Often they return to their homeland as missionaries and start underground churches.

Since it is considered a disgrace—tantamount to a crime—to convert to Christianity, Arab Christians are earnest in their faith. A tiny minority in a Muslim culture of eight hundred million worldwide, they accept formidable odds in committing their lives to Christ. This explains the deep secrecy of the underground church, which survives in decidedly hostile soil.

In the twentieth century, Christianity is perceived largely as a Western phenomenon in spite of its origins in the ancestral home of both Arabs and Jews. That it takes root against all odds in the Islamic Middle East is a miracle of grace that has had a thousand counterparts throughout the centuries since twelve unlettered men and a former Pharisee turned the world upside down.

As a young Christian from India, I went to the United Arab Emirates (U.A.E.) along with many of my countrymen to seek employment. There I determined to be a faithful witness for Christ—no matter the risk. In the coming pages you will discover what it costs to follow Christ in a culture at fierce enmity with our Lord, and you will witness the sacrifice of those who dare to spread the gospel of Christ under the ever-watchful eye of the crescent moon.

CHAPTER 1

Under Arrest

The police have come!"

With these ominous words my wife greeted me as I returned home from work at 11 a.m.

"George John?" an officer standing near the door scowled. I nodded reluctantly.

"You are under arrest!"

The stern tone of the officer told me it was useless to ask why. Even so, I had little doubt as to what the charges would be.

My wife and I had known that this moment might come any day, but the reality of finding two police officers waiting for me in my home jolted me nonetheless.

I hurried to embrace my wife as she burst into tears. My eyes longingly searched the faces of my two little girls. I wondered if I would ever see them again.

Impatient with my farewells, the officers shoved me through the door and toward a van. Although the police headquarters in Sharjah was only a mile away, I traveled an impassable psychological distance from the peace and love of my home to the uncertainty and brutality of prison. I knew that my faith would be tested.

Enduring the Test

At headquarters, the officers ushered me into a room and told me to sit. For several hours I sat in silence under the guard of two policemen. I imagined what my family must be going through, wanting to comfort them. I fought the rising anxiety over what might happen to me, wondering if I would be able to stand firm and suffer for my Lord. Such thoughts circled round and round interminably, heightened by the realization that I might never see my family again.

Finally, at 4 p.m., I was marched down a long corridor to a small room and made to sit on the floor in front of toilets filled with human waste. A guard set a dish of food beside me. But the stench was so overpowering I could scarcely breathe, let alone eat. Feeling sick to my stomach, I pushed the food away.

"Eat it!" the guard snarled. His tone threatened "or else."

Fearing physical torture, I gagged it down. This was my first punishment. I endured the foul odors for more than five hours before I was summoned back to the first room. Although relieved to be away from the stench of the toilets, I felt a growing sense of apprehension at the sight of another man being shoved into a cell.

He had been selling "pan" or betel leaves—a forbidden drug chewed with tobacco.

Realizing the intensity of torture in such a place, I thought of Jesus being beaten for me two thousand years ago. The reality of what my Savior had endured took on a new dimension as I watched the beating from where I sat—probably a deliberate ploy. Blood and water dripped from the nose of the victim, who appeared about to pass out.

If this is how they treat a minor offense, what will they do to me? I shuddered. My "crime" was far greater in the eyes of the law. In an Arab country where Islam is protected and Christianity is hated, I had dared to smuggle the Word of God, an enterprise strictly prohibited by the law of the land. That offense, I knew, was heinous in the eyes of my Muslim captors.

Soon an officer marched me to the same cell. Trembling uncontrollably, I lifted my eyes heavenward and prayed for Jesus' help. A blow from behind propelled me further into the room. But my prayer was answered, in what can only be described as a miracle. This was the only blow I was to receive. God saved me from being beaten to a pulp like my predecessor. I thanked the Lord for His unfailing presence and providence.

Next I was taken to the office of Police Inspector Khalifa, a young, handsome Arab who was to be my interrogator.

"Sit down!" he ordered, looking up from a sheaf of papers containing the charges he had prepared.

"I have a record of all of your offenses. John Panicker, your co-worker, frankly admitted everything!" He eyed me steadily to let that sink in.

"I understand that you were getting the addresses of the noble citizens of our land from our country's telephone directory and mailing them your religious materials. It is evident that you were importing gospel tracts from America into the U.A.E. in order to spread your religion here."

Khalifa leaned forward and narrowed his eyes. "This is an open violation of the law. You were the one who brought all the religious literature from India. So much is already proven against you. I cannot believe a gentleman such as you would indulge in such activities! Why did you do all these things? Answer my questions honestly."

Though Khalifa spoke and acted like a gentleman, I could not believe that my Christian brother John Panicker had admitted everything to him. I was sure he would never betray me. Recognizing the tactics, I replied carefully.

Defending the Faith

"I am a Christian. The words of the Bible are the basis of my faith. The Scriptures teach what a

Christian should do. I am bound to obey the teachings of the Bible. One of them says that a Christian should go all over the world and proclaim the gospel of Jesus Christ. This is what I tried to do."

Khalifa held up the Koran and asked me to show him such a teaching of "Isa Nabi" (Prophet Jesus) in his holy book.

I sat forward and pointed at the Koran. "That is not the Bible which contains the Word of God. It is only a book of moral principles taught by the prophet Mohammed. It is not the Bible, the Word of God given to mankind. The Koran is not a book of that kind!"

His face lit up with anger. Grabbing a cane, he raised it to beat me but quickly restrained himself. "We are about the same age and are both educated. I was educated in London. Therefore I won't beat someone like you." His anger faded as he added matter-of-factly, "I am not going to beat you."

I seized the moment. "I would like to explain my position."

He nodded.

I related my testimony, beginning with how I was saved through the blood of Jesus Christ. "Today I stand before you as a criminal. I am here only because I obeyed a commandment from the Holy Bible. I receive light from Jesus Christ, and I shall try to radiate this light to others wherever I am."

Suddenly I remembered the words of the apostle John when he was in exile on the island of Patmos and repeated them out loud: "I was [arrested] because of the word of God and the testimony of Jesus" (Revelation 1:9).

My testimony took about an hour. The inspector listened with full attention and recorded what I said. But what he heard was that I had tried to do the unthinkable: I had proclaimed the gospel in order to convert Muslims to Christianity!

He shook his head. "Maybe you are sincere, but you are a criminal before the law of Islam and the law of this Muslim country. Such a criminal cannot escape the death penalty!"

He paused, and I thought he regarded me sympathetically. "Listen to me," he offered, "if you accept Islam and become a Muslim, admitting your guilt and pleading for mercy, you may escape capital punishment. You may have only a few years of imprisonment, and then you will be able to live out your life in this world!"

No Regrets

"Become a Muslim!" I almost shouted. "Admit that I am guilty and thereby betray my Lord Jesus Christ—my Savior Jesus Christ, who laid down His life for me? No, never! I shall not give up my eternal life in order to escape a momentary death. I will not forsake my Lord Jesus Christ, who gave me eternal life. He died for me.

I am ready to die for Him. I have no regret for what I did."

After a prolonged pause, Inspector Khalifa wrote on the charge sheet, "The accused does not regret his guilt." Handing me a pen, he spoke flatly. "Sign it."

I stood and leaned over the form on his desk, putting my signature to what could be my death warrant.

Around 10 o'clock that night I was escorted to a dark prison cell on the bottom floor of a building adjacent to the four-story police head-quarters. I could not have imagined such horror.

The door was fifteen inches thick. Beyond it I could see the road leading to my home through a barred window. I felt sickened by the thought that tonight I would not be with my family shar-ing their love, praying with them, and enjoying the cleanliness and warmth of our small place. So much had happened in the past twelve hours! Yet we had always known we could be separated, and we had counted ourselves worthy of suffer-ing for the name of the Lord.

I was shoved into a cell with thirty criminals. This night I would begin to know a little bit about what hell must be like. The stench was over-powering. The latrine, built in the ground along one of the walls, had long since overflowed its small confines, and the waste simply emptied into the cell. I was dumbfounded to discover that it reached midway between our ankles and our knees.

Like all other prisoners, I had been given two blankets. But these were not ordinary blankets. They felt and smelled more like lumps of dung. In an effort to protect themselves from the overflowing filth, the prisoners had used their blankets to build a wall against the rising tide of human waste. Behind this makeshift wall, they stretched out as best they could to rest. I did the same, then put the other folded blanket on the wretched floor and sat on it.

One by one the other prisoners began to ask me questions. What had I done? What was my crime? As if in a stupor, I could not open my mouth. I sat like someone deaf and dumb. Even my breathing was labored. When I failed to answer, my cellmates began to heap verbal abuses on me.

Although my body ached with fatigue, and I felt exhausted from the emotional drain of the previous hours, I could not sleep. The prisoners sang filthy songs, told off-color jokes, and recounted tales of their misadventures and villainous behavior.

This must be what men will do in hell, I judged. These were men without God, men who seemingly had nothing of God in them. *How can such individuals ever repent of their evil ways? Would they even want to repent?* Their hearts, I knew, had been hardened, and they were chronic criminals.

Prisons like this, I decided, would never reform them.

During that long night, my mind seemed to lose consciousness, escaping on wings of memory to the events of my past.

CHAPTER 2

From the Beginning

Born in 1951 in Bombay, India, I was given my Christian name in the Good House Catholic Church. Eventually, when my family grew to five girls and two boys, my father sent us with our mother to her native state of Kerala, where he continued to support us on his slender wages.

At the age of sixteen, I passed my secondary examination, and while I would have loved to continue my education, I was forced to seek work to help support the family. Packing my graduation certificate and my one change of clothes in an old newspaper, I set out by bus and train on the three-day journey back to Bombay, where I joined my father.

After working for a while in a motor bicycle factory, owned by demon-worshippers who underpaid and abused me, I tried to join the merchant navy. But I was rejected because I lacked the 200 rupees for initial expenses. From there my life took a downturn as I fell into the company of drunkards and ne'er-do-wells. I stole from my father, who didn't understand my behavior, and lived by the power of a knife that I carried.

With the wicked, I became wicked, and for six years my life drifted aimlessly.

Then, in the providence of God, I walked into a church frequented by some of my countrymen. I recognized twin brothers, who had been my neighbors, praying. Discovering that they lived close by, I welcomed them as friends, and life took a gradual upturn.

My life began to change as a result of their friendship. The twins lived a clean life, used decent language, and studied the Bible regularly. From the light of the lamp that shone on their Bible, I would light my cigarette as they read verse after verse. Though I loved to read world-famous books by philosophers, statesmen, and literary figures, never had I heard such teachings as they shared with me from the Word of God. As a Catholic, I assumed that the Bible was only for the priests. It never occurred to me to open its pages.

My desire to learn the truths of the Bible increased steadily. Soon, because of the changed lives of the brothers and the power of God's Word, I felt convicted of my sins.

I sought answers to my many questions about Christianity through the lives and testimonies of faithful Christian workers and evangelists. Among them was the biography of P. C. George, who with his sister Leyamma devoted his whole life to the service of the desolate and sick in South India.

My heart was deeply touched by one particular story about a Hindu woman, Lakshmi. She had been forsaken by her husband and rejected by her daughter. Desolate, Lakshmi became seriously ill and took to bed, unable to move. Without hope, she decided to drag herself out to the road to be crushed under the wheels of a passing vehicle.

By the grace of God, Brother George happened by, took pity on the wretched woman, lifted her paralyzed body into a cart, and pulled it himself to the home for the desolate that he and his sister ran by faith. Here Leyamma gently cared for the desperate woman.

Lakshmi, assuming the women who ministered to her were paid for their services, often complained about their care. Then one day she heard them praying and realized that they had gone without food for days in order to feed her and the desolate orphans for whom they cared. Overwhelmed by the love of Christ in their lives, Lakshmi's heart broke, and she cried bitterly over her ungrateful attitude. Soon she received Jesus Christ and found peace in her soul. She died with a blessed hope.

I came to understand that the true love of Christ causes a transformation in human minds and souls. Jesus, I learned, is the very incarnation of love. Marxism, Leninism, Maoism, and

Communism bow before the power of His love. These "isms" promised a glorious "utopia," but they could not recreate the great love of Christ proven on Calvary. By accepting this love, the individual is transformed into a life of holiness, righteousness, truth, and benevolence. This can lead to the reformation of the community. Truly, this was a revolution of love.

How I longed for such love in my life! Jesus, I learned, was not a mere historical figure. The revelation that He is alive and lives for me today opened my heart and removed my blindness. I opened my heart to Him, just as I understood He was preparing a home for me.

Repenting of my past with tears and confessing my sins, I felt the heavy burden roll away, and I was born again according to John 3:3. As I surrendered myself at the feet of Christ, I made an irrevocable covenant: My life would be totally dedicated to Him and His gospel forever...

Somehow that memory gave me solace as I sat in the squalor of my cell in Sharjah. I had indeed become a new man the day I had received Christ. Determined to remain faithful to His gospel even in this ordeal, my mind once again wandered to my early years of Christian life.

In December 1973, I was baptized in water—a born-again Christian from a Roman Catholic family in a Hindu country! Little did I know what lay ahead.

The next three and a half years were a time of great trial. After my conversion, I brought my mother and siblings back from Kerala to live in Bombay. However, my father reacted with hostility to my conversion and after beating and starving me, he finally expelled me from home.

A friend opened up his home, giving me a roof over my head but nothing more. He worked in a training program earning a few rupees, but his lunch bag was always empty and he had only one pair of pants and a shirt to his name.

Despite these circumstances, my faith in God and my love for Him never wavered—though one evening as I sat alone on a terrace, terrible hunger and fatigue afflicted me. *What am I going to do?* I wondered. *I don't have a job. How can I make a living?* I craved direction from the Lord for my life.

I felt restless. God had placed a great vision in my heart for serving Him, but why was my situation so hopeless? Then I remembered the words of Jesus, "Do not worry, saying, 'What shall we eat?' or 'What shall we drink?' or 'What shall we wear?' For…your heavenly Father knows that you need them" (Matthew 6:31,32).

Though darkness was falling, it seemed that the darker the night became, the greater the light grew in my heart as a result of that Scripture. Hope for my future returned.

To the Wilderness of the Gulf

After a few weeks, my spiritual brother, Thomas John, told me of a vacancy in the A & P Company in the United Arab Emirates. I felt elated. Another friend had already help me get a passport. I scheduled an interview with A & P for the next day.

I was there on time, but a long queue of applicants was waiting. I felt embarrassed to push myself into the line but knew the job would be taken before many had been interviewed. Suddenly a man near the front, realizing he was not qualified for the job, left his position and pushed me into his place! I was now fourth in line. The first three men were unfit for the job, and I was hired.

In April 1977, I started work in the state of Dubai, one of seven in the U.A.E.[1] For a year I worked for A & P, under conditions of great hardship that I still shudder to remember. We were forced to work from six in the morning until ten at night. Our barracks had no water, no electricity, not even a lavatory. After our long hours of work, we had to prepare our own food

---

[1] The United Arab Emirates consists of seven states on the toe of the peninsula that juts into the Arabian Gulf: Abu Dhabi, Dubai, Sharjah, Fujeirah, Ras-Al-Khaima, Umm-Al-Quaiwan, and Ajman. Each state is ruled by a sheik, and all seven together have a federal government. The ministries of health, defense, and post and telegraph are all under the central government.

and then sleep on steel frame cots with only a cloth sheet as cover.

When we could stand no more, the Indians organized and appointed me to lead a demonstration and boycott against the company. Eventually the authorities gave in to our demands.

As life began to improve, my heart overflowed with gratitude. How well I remember those days when I gradually stepped from gray poverty into days of plenty. It felt good to have some rupees in my pocket. Even so, the absence of Christian fellowship grieved me.

The Lord knew my heart's desire. One day I met a stranger at the Thermak Camp in Sharjah who I soon discovered was a believer. I greatly rejoiced as Varghese and I began to pray together.

While working at the A & P, I met Sivadasan, a fellow Indian who was possessed with a demon. Suicidal, he tried to jump into the sea to end his life. But God had other plans. I was able to save him from the water and pray for him. Miraculously, he was delivered from demon possession and received Jesus Christ as his personal Savior. Later, we lived together in a villa in Sharjah Rolla. Our life there was very happy.

It was wonderful to see my contacts with other believers increase. I had not been in Sharjah very long when I met Brother Solomon, a servant of God with the zeal of an evangelist. When I went to a labor camp for gospel work, he also went to proclaim the gospel to the inmates. Eventually we rented a big house in which to conduct worship services. As personal evangelism and Christian fellowship continued, we prayed that our ministry would increase. Many believed and were baptized in the sea near the palace of the sheik. Our fellowship grew rapidly. Eventually, I obtained a good job with good salary in the international airport of Dubai…

Now, sitting in my cell in Sharjah, I recalled those days with joy. My mind turned to the conversion of a hippie named Henk. A caricature of a man, he was striving for peace of mind. He had become a disciple of a Hindu monk and was traveling illegally on a Japanese ship to join his master in India. The ship had stopped at a U.A.E. port for repairs, and he had disembarked. Hungry and dirty, he was wandering aimlessly when we met him and introduced him to the love of Christ.

Henk quickly realized his need for salvation of the soul and peace of mind. He raised no barriers to receiving Jesus Christ and was baptized in water. He became a true disciple of Jesus, and the last I knew he was proclaiming the gospel somewhere in Europe.

Gospel Work Among the Arabs

Christians are not few in the Arab countries, but their main goal is to amass wealth and not to share the treasures of heaven. It had occurred to me one day that I might be among them.

What am I doing to further the gospel while earning Persian dinars? I had asked myself. *Is my heart set on mundane riches or heavenly wealth? Where will the lust for life lead me? What about my motives?*

I decided then to dedicate myself totally to God and laid my life at His feet. Like St. Paul, I knew what was most important in my life: "One thing I do: Forgetting what is behind and straining toward what is ahead, I press on toward the goal to win the prize for which God has called me heavenward in Christ Jesus" (Philippians 3:13,14).

Many friends did not approve. Proclaiming the gospel in the land of Arabs was forbidden and dangerous, they protested. But I thanked God for my two Christian brothers, Solomon and John Panicker, who supported my decision.

Again remembering Police Inspector Khalifa's charge that Brother Panicker had betrayed me, I shook my head. A dedicated Christian witness, he would not have done such a thing. I recalled his conversion experience.

Admitted to Almaktom Hospital in Dubai for snakebite, John Panicker met Brother Solomon, who was working there. Brother Solomon and I decided to visit this gentleman together. A member of an Orthodox community, Panicker would never have welcomed an evangelist alone.

We shared the good news of salvation in Jesus and urged him to receive Christ. After a lengthy argument and talk about the doctrines of the Bible, we convinced him of his need for salvation. By the grace of God, Mr. Panicker and his family accepted the Lord in one day. Gradually the Panicker family grew in their knowledge of God's Word and had remained steadfast in their Christian faith.

Brother Solomon and I knew the Arabs hated Christianity. But the Spirit of the Lord urged us to proclaim the gospel of Jesus Christ in this Muslim country nevertheless, and soon John Panicker joined us in our mission.

The din of the other prisoners seemed to fade into mere shadows as I thought of the challenges we faced in sharing the gospel.

The name of Christ is forbidden in Arabian lands. The Arabs would acknowledge "Isa Nabi" (Jesus the prophet) as a prophet, but they would never accept Him as the Son of God and the Savior of the world.

Muslims admit that Jesus Christ once lived on earth, but only because the historical truth of Christianity cannot be denied. Since the Jews are anathema to the Arabs, and Jesus was a Jew, He is an object of contempt to them.

This attitude is rooted in biblical history. Since the genealogy of Scripture refers to "Jacob, the son of Isaac, the son of Abraham," the Jews trace their ancestry to Abraham from Isaac through Jacob. The Arabs establish their right in Ishmael.

The Jews claim Isaac as the rightful heir of Abraham because Ishmael was born the son of Abraham's maid and therefore not the legal inheritor. The Arabs, on the other hand, justify their claim in the fact that Ishmael was the eldest son of "Ibrahme Nabi" (Abraham) and so give primacy to the genealogy of Ishmael.

Because of this dispute, Jews and Christians are looked down upon in Muslim countries. Neither a Jew nor a Christian is permitted to own even an inch of land—even though it was the Christianized Western nations that dug oil wells and established oil companies, thereby enriching Arabs who had been the slaves of poverty.

From the time I dedicated my life to Christ, spreading His gospel among the Arabs was my constant thought. Jesus had told His followers, "Go into all the world and preach the good news to all creation" (Mark 16:15). Jesus did not command, "Go into all the world except the Arab nations." He said, "Go into *all* the world." The apostle Paul said, "I thank my God through Jesus Christ for all of you, because your faith is being reported all over the world" (Romans 1:8). Shouldn't I follow my Lord's explicit command? Shouldn't I fulfill the vow I had taken? Do the servants of the Lord realize the implications of the "whole world"? These questions weighed heavily upon me.

Because Arab intolerance of faiths other than Islam is undergirded by the cruel punishment of non-Muslim religious workers, most Christians have shied from even thinking of gospel work among the Arabs.

I had heard of an English missionary, for example, who preached the gospel openly in the streets of Deira, Dubai. He was arrested immediately and never came out of prison. He never saw the sun again. I also knew of a Pakistani Christian who converted an Arab to Christianity. They both had to pay with their lives for their faith in Jesus. I wondered what fate awaited me.

In Muslim countries, the Koran is the law of the land. Penalties for violating the law are cruel. A thief, for example, can lose his hand. Adulterers are punished by being beheaded, stoned to death, or shot in a public place. The penalty for drug abuse can be plucking out the nails of the hands and feet. But those who work against Islam are treated even more cruelly.

In my cell in Sharjah, I wondered if I would have to live out my life in its squalor—or did another fate await me? One thing was certain. If necessary, I was willing to sacrifice my life for my Savior.

Because the Koran is inferior to the Bible in both style and content, Arabs are afraid to let the Bible into their lands. They know that if people were permitted to read the Holy Bible, they would leave Islam and accept Christianity. Thus by every means possible, Muslims prevent the teachings of Christ and the Holy Bible from entering their territories. According to history, Islam was established by the sword. Under such conditions, my friends and I found it very dangerous to promote the gospel of Christ among the Arabs.

Fully aware of the consequences, we three—Brothers Solomon, Panicker, and I—had made plans for evangelizing this most difficult part of the world. We decided to lay down our lives if necessary to bring the bread of life to this hostile country.

Meeting in secret, we discussed how we could smuggle in the New Testament and other Christian literature in the Arabic language. We vowed that if any of us were caught, we would never betray the others—even at the point of death—so that the work could still be carried out until all of us were caught. This is how I knew Khalifa's claim that Panicker betrayed me was a mere ploy to demoralize and weaken me.

All of our moves had to be carefully considered and kept absolutely secret. A single, unwise act might jeopardize the whole mission and get us killed. Therefore, we agreed not to mention this work except among ourselves. Our mission must not end in a day. It must have a long life—at least a couple of years so that we could distribute the heavenly manna to the perishing and hungry souls.

Cautiously we embarked upon our secret operation.

Early Preparations

Obtaining Gospels and Christian pamphlets in Arabic took careful planning, since none were printed in Muslim countries. We had to purchase them from America and have them shipped to Bombay. From there, we planned to transport the literature to the Arabian Gulf.

I decided to go to Bombay and smuggle some bundles on a flight to Dubai. Since I was a member of the airport staff, I could escape customs without being checked.

In spite of all precautions, however, I found myself gripped by horrible fears on my initial trip. Importing Christian literature, I knew, was a mortal "crime" and I didn't even want to contemplate the penalty. But Jesus had given the Great Commission, and I felt assured that He would oversee my operation.

While they were Trucial States under British protection, these Arab territories offered possibilities for gospel work. Some Americans opened mission hospitals in Sharjah and Al-Ain to reach the local people for Christ. But the sad truth is, they did not exploit all the possibilities for evangelization. Although they brought in Gospel portions in Arabic, most of the material lay on storage shelves unused. The opportunity

passed when the country became an independent federation of Arab states in 1971.

We found the old literature and collected all
that had not been eaten by white ants. Meanwhile, we prayed that God would open up a way
to distribute His Word. Such a work required not
only courage but sound strategy. We determined
to proceed carefully and tactfully so that our
work would go unhindered.

We decided that any Arab confronted with
the gospel should first reflect on it, then come
to accept Jesus Christ as his personal Savior, and
eventually become an apostle to his own land.
We prayed that the seed we were sowing would
bear fruit a hundredfold.

We continued to seek God's guidance
through prayer until a way to spread the gospel
opened up before us. Although it had its
dangers, we decided the plan was heaven-sent.
We simply would use a telephone directory,
copying down all the addresses of Arabs every-
where.

Within weeks the noble citizens of all seven
states of the U.A.E. began to receive the bread
of life from different places within the country...

CHAPTER 3

Spies for Christ

Despite the agony I suffered in my prison cell in Sharjah, I could not help but smile triumphantly at the wisdom of our Lord in penetrating even the most difficult places of the world. His plan was ingenious, and the thought that Solomon, Panicker, and I were spies for the Lord bolstered my courage and strengthened my resolve.

After enclosing a Gospel portion in each stamped, addressed envelope, we had laid hands on them and prayed that each would bear fruit. Then the three of us divided up the bundles and headed for three different states. At an appointed time, we mailed our packages from different post offices to all seven states.

For four years we successfully smuggled the gospel into hostile territory. Eventually, however, we learned that some fanatical Muslims who had received our mail were giving information to the authorities.

At first they prohibited all Christian periodicals from entering the country. Then they were astonished to see that the forbidden material was coming from within the country. As a result, the government began a serious investigation and tightened security. We noticed changes in laws regarding immigration, customs, and the importation of foreign goods. Print shops were checked, and the authorities even began to suspect the American CIA and the Israeli Mossad (secret police) of exploiting the Muslim religion.

If the Arabs fear anything, it is the CIA and the Mossad. If a palm tree falls down, it is because the CIA is engaging in biological warfare. If a truck collides with another vehicle, this is sabotage by Mossad terrorists.

And so the authorities intensified their search for the spies of Christ. With great care, we three stepped up our work, realizing that we had little time left for our activities. Gospel stickers showed up in such unlikely places as the doorsteps of Arab offices and on their cars. If a car window was slightly open, we inserted a New Testament. We placed gospel packets as gifts at the gates of Arab homes. We tucked Bibles into the baggage that passed through the airport. And we discretely stuffed pamphlets containing Jesus' teachings into the bags of people returning from the hospital.

Some may ask: Is it right to smuggle the gospel into a country if it is against the law of that land? Can a Christian break the law when the

Bible says he should be submissive to "every authority instituted among men: whether to the king, as the supreme authority, or to governors, who are sent by him to punish those who do wrong and to commend those who do right" (1 Peter 2:13,14)?

Such questions can be answered. The gospel of Christ has always faced opposition. From the beginning, the early Christians suffered intense persecution and many became martyrs for the sake of the gospel.

The message of Christ is resisted and rejected in this world because the Bible says the whole world lies under Satan's control. God's Word calls him "the god of this world." Paul himself wrote, "Our struggle is not against flesh and blood, but against the rulers, against the authorities, against the powers of this dark world and against the spiritual forces of evil in the heavenly realms" (Ephesians 6:12).

Gospel work is a war between God and Satan, light and darkness, righteousness and evil. Since it is a spiritual warfare between two celestial powers, the law of any nation stopping the spread of the gospel is not applicable. The liberating power of the kingdom of God is the gospel. The forces of darkness reject it because they are determined to keep people captive.

The devil and his forces can only be defeated by the light of God's Word. But until Satan's captives realize that the gospel is light and life to all who receive it, they will continue to resist.

In this spiritual warfare, the children of light can expect to find themselves engaged in the battle as soldiers, agents, spies, and guerrilla fighters. Their duty is to penetrate spiritual darkness with heavenly light, to love where there is hate, to bring food to the hungry, to liberate all who will listen from the bondage of Satan. They must confront the principalities and powers of another sphere with unfaltering boldness and heaven-inspired strategy.

Therefore, where the gospel is not welcomed, it must be spread in secret. Smuggling becomes a way of fulfilling the gospel imperative.

True, a Christian must be a good citizen and obey his country's laws. But when the regulations of the state conflict with the laws of God, a Christian has to draw the line. His higher calling must take precedence. He must obey God rather than man (Acts 5:29).

The three Hebrew men who were thrown into the fiery furnace—Shadrach, Meshach, and Abednego—were loyal to the king until he demanded that they deny their faith. In breaking his commands, they were ready to become martyrs.

To the questions about smuggling I would reply, "Judge for yourselves whether it is right in God's sight to obey you (man) rather than God.

For we cannot help speaking about what we have seen and heard" (Acts 4:19,20).

A true Christian will never bow before any law that forbids him to share his faith or act contrary to it. For such conviction, I was willing to die.

The Spies Arrested

In spite of the increasing vigilance of the authorities, nothing happened. We had been careful, even skillful. Then one night God gave me a vision that we were arrested by the U.A.E. police. In three days the dream came true.

We three "spies" were living in a four-story building. Brother Solomon and his family occupied an apartment across the hall from Brother Panicker and his wife. My family and I lived on the top floor.

In their search for the source of the Christian literature, the secret police focused mainly on the Christians from America, Britain, Lebanon, and Palestine. Somehow they never suspected that Indians from a Hindu nation would be involved in such work. But eventually the spying eyes of the investigators fell upon us. After a long, detailed search, a band of police surrounded our building.

It was a holiday. The police and agents from the criminal branch first raided the apartment of Brother Solomon. Since he and his wife were not home, they carried his brother Jacob off to police headquarters. When Monsy, a Christian brother, knocked on Solomon's door, he too was taken into custody. Observing through a peephole what was taking place, Brother Panicker's wife slipped out of her apartment and ran up to mine.

"There are Arabs in Solomon's house." She was breathless with fear. "They took Jacob away. I heard them breaking into cupboards as they ransacked the apartment."

I started to run down to Solomon's place, but my wife stopped me.

"It might be about the gospel work," she cautioned.

Because our wives were aware of our secret mission, I listened to her warning and thought for a moment. My room contained many gospel packets, which I took to the washroom and covered with a bedsheet. Then I went down to the second floor and used a neighbor's telephone to call Brother Panicker at his work. "John, the police are raiding Solomon's apartment. Jacob has been arrested and taken away." I also told him about Monsy, who was being held hostage, and that I was going to investigate further what was happening.

"Be very careful," John cautioned.

"I will be very wise and just pretend that I am a stranger," I assured him. "If I'm caught, I will never betray our mission. I would rather die." I told Panicker to find Solomon and his wife and inform them to act wisely.

In moments I was at Solomon's door knocking. The police opened the door. Acting surprised, I asked in Arabic, "Su-hata?" (What is the matter?) Saying they were the police, they asked me to come in. Brother Monsy was sitting in the living room looking pale and frightened. Two policemen were guarding him. Since he knew nothing, he was thoroughly confused.

Speaking in broken Arabic and Urdu, I told the police I was a friend of Solomon's and had just come to see him.

"Then you shall not go out until Solomon returns," an official dressed in civilian clothes huffed. "We have to arrest him and his group for working against Islam."

I decided to keep quiet. Sitting on a chair next to Monsy, I spoke to him in low tones in our mother tongue, comforting him. Meanwhile, the police continued to ransack the rooms—moving furniture, digging into cupboards and closets, even the oven, and tearing up the carpet—in search of more literature and evidence. As they scoured the apartment, one of the Arab policemen guarding Monsy read some of the literature eagerly. Soon the police had collected thousands of gospel tracts, tapes, and other literature in the living room. Suddenly noticing my conversation with Monsy, the official in charge ordered me to stop talking to him.

Finally, the police contacted headquarters by wireless, informing them about me and Monsy. They received orders to take us to the police station. As we left under guard, my wife who was watching from the balcony started to cry and run down after me. I gestured for her not to come down just as Mrs. Panicker grabbed her and escorted her back into our apartment.

By the grace of God, the police did not observe this bit of drama.

At the Sharjah police station Monsy and I were told that we could not be released until Solomon and his companions were arrested. If they had thought to ask my name and my address, they could have arrested the main culprit they were seeking. I thanked God for their indifference and stupidity.

The news of our arrest spread like wildfire among the Indian Christians and soon traveled across the country. All the believers were panic-stricken. When someone telephoned, asking what had happened to us, they were almost afraid to give a warning, fearful that their lines might be tapped. Many hid their Bibles and Christian books.

Solomon and his wife returned home, fully aware of the grimness of their situation. On the way, Solomon met his friend Al Asaili, a wealthy man who was a friend of the sheik of Sharjah. Since Al Asaili was a compassionate man, Solomon hoped that his intimacy with the ruler would save us. But Al Asaili's appeal was turned down by senior police officials from the Federal Government. Furthermore, he was told not to interfere in this matter since we were conspiring against the religion of Islam.

Soon Solomon and his wife were with us in the same room at the Sharjah police headquarters. But when Monsy opened his mouth to say something to his friend, a policeman struck him on the head with a wireless telephone. "Why did you do that? That man is innocent!" I demanded and received the same blow in reply.

Half an hour later, when Solomon and his wife were taken to different cells, we overheard the names "George John, John Panicker, and Solomon Thomas." By then I was sure the police knew the whole story of our secret mission.

Somehow Monsy and I were released with warnings not to go to the area where we were picked up. I shook my head pretending innocence, and the two of us went our separate ways. I reached home by taxi, expecting a large crowd, but the place was desolate. I was consoled by the words of the psalmist, "Do not be far from me, for trouble is near and there is no one to help" (Psalm 22:11).

After comforting my wife, I went to the home of her uncle, Brother K. M. Samuel, for fellowship and prayer. Many anxious believers had assembled there to learn about us. John Panicker also joined me. When we revealed our secret labor for the gospel, they became frightened because the names of those in our fellowship had been confiscated by the police in the raid. Everyone assumed that all would be arrested.

I reassured them that only the three of us who had distributed the literature would be arrested. I encouraged our brethren to pray for us, reminding them that the Lord had allowed me to slip through the hands of the enemy so that I could strengthen their hands.

When we returned home, the police were guarding Solomon's apartment. Looking the other way, Panicker and I crept to our rooms. That night I stayed up with my family in the living room. My innocent children—Sarah, two, and Esther, just ten months—sensed trouble as they saw tears on their mother's face. But they felt safe in our laps.

Late that night, Mrs. Panicker knocked on our front door weeping. "Two policemen just took my husband away," she choked. My wife wrapped a comforting arm around her as we walked with her down to her apartment and stayed in her living room. I tried to encourage her, knowing that the police would soon come back and take me, too.

That night my mind pitched and rolled like a ship in a storm. Thinking about my beloved brothers Solomon, Jacob, and Panicker, and Sister Leelamma who were already in police custody, I wondered what tribulation I would face. What punishment would be in store for all of us?

Trying to restrain my trembling, I gave my wife directions for the future, gently explaining what to do if I were sentenced to death or did not return for long years. Inside I had little hope, and I could sense that my wife didn't either.

"If I return after many years," I ventured, holding her closer, "will you wait for me? And if I don't, will we meet in that eternal morning on the other side?"

She trembled and wept bitterly, burying her face in my chest. It was better to be silent about some things.

Morning dawned, and no one came to arrest me. Waiting had been the hardest.

Taking advantage of my brief liberty, I went to the office to say goodbye to my friends and to explain what was happening. My superior, Mr. Pasha, showed great compassion for me and suggested a way of escape—cross the border illegally. I told him my moral standing would not permit me to do so.

Soon I left the office in the Dubai airport and went to see my wife's cousin, Joyce, and her husband, Babu. Using their telephone, I contacted all my friends and relatives. I also talked to my cousin, Babychan, who was a business partner with an Arab.

Greatly troubled, he came immediately. "You must leave the country right away," he urged. "I can get you aboard a cargo plane that transports meat from India."

I refused. "How can I be a coward and flee while my brothers are in prison? How can I leave behind my wife and children in this hostile country? They would be taken hostages to bring me back."

Babychan tried hard to persuade me, but I found steady determination in the words of Paul, "Why are you weeping and breaking my heart? I am ready not only to be bound, but also to die in Jerusalem for the name of the Lord Jesus" (Acts 21:13).

Giving up, Babychan drove me home in his car, dropping me nearby. "I shall do my best to get you out of prison very soon," he consoled quietly.

"Thank you, Babychan. I know you will try." I walked briskly toward my apartment as my wife ran out to me.

"The police officers have come . . ." Her voice trailed into helpless quietness.

As expected, I was arrested . . .

The stir of men adding to the vile odors of my cell jerked me back to the present. For a moment it seemed that my wife and children were part of a distant past that was gone except in memory. Bracing myself so I would not slide deeper into the waste around me, I slipped into a troubled sleep.

CHAPTER 4

Maranatha

In the morning, I found myself lying in the filthy yellowish water flowing from the latrine. My body was smeared all over with fecal matter, almost as if I had been dipped in human waste, and my hair was sticky and moist. The foul smell and the degrading contamination were beneath human dignity. Standing up, I struggled to breathe. *Can hell be worse than this?* I shuddered.

Smothered in putrefaction, I quickly surveyed the cell—four Indians from Kerala, some Pakistani nationals, and Arabs. I stood silently for a moment, retreating further into myself. Not satisfied with their taunts of the night before, some of the prisoners again began to assault me with their degrading questions and obscene stories. I had tuned out their verbal abuses before by focusing on the events that had led me to this unspeakable hell. Now, however, I began to face reality.

When the guard came with our food, the prisoners lunged at their portions like ravenous animals. Breakfast consisted of cheese and cuppoose (a kind of pita bread) and sulaimani (sour tea). Those who had a container would receive tea. Over time, older prisoners had managed to salvage the broken half of a bottle or a used coke can as a container, but I had nothing. My thirst was great. Suddenly Judges 7:6 flashed into my mind, "Three hundred men lapped with their hands to their mouths."

Quickly, I cupped my hands and stretched them out. The hot sulaimani burned my flesh, but I did not spill a drop. I remembered that my Lord thirsted on the cross and had nothing to drink.

Later a guard took me to another cell, where I paced alone in the darkness. On my way, I saw John Panicker in a cell adjacent to mine. I paused for a moment, and we peered into one another's eyes. He had been arrested a day earlier. This was our first meeting after those fateful events.

During my second night, I could hardly sit or stand or lie down. I felt swallowed up in desolation, gripped in an unexplainable restlessness, isolated in mental torture, totally exhausted but unable to even close my eyes.

No prayer came to my mind, no chorus to my lips. I craved for fellowship, my spirit crying out for a smiling face or a word of comfort. But my eyes could see only an unsmiling, stern jailer sitting at a table under a dim light. My ears could hear only the sounds of groaning, slumbering prisoners.

Finally, refusing to defile my somewhat clean cell, I called to the guard, "Please, take me to the toilet!" With his gun plainly visible, he reluctantly escorted me to the other end of the corridor.

Again I peeked into Brother Panicker's cell. He was still there! With a sudden burst of courage, I cried, "Maranatha!" (Our Lord comes!)

From deep inside the cell, Panicker's voice echoed the wonderful word. "Maranatha!" I saw my beloved brother in Christ—though faintly—and felt a joy in my soul such as no other fellowship could ever give. Jesus was with us. What comfort came to me and to my brother, for this word gave reason and purpose to our being in the midst of the insanity surrounding us. Great was the joy of Christian fellowship.

Earlier a Pakistani had asked me, "Sab, Kya ap ek pathiri hei?" (Are you an evangelist? How did you come to this prison?) Somehow I managed to tell him, "God sent me here to tell the gospel to you." At the time I wondered how much he could understand the implications of those words. But now, after hearing "Maranatha," I understood much better myself!

In Solitary Confinement

Soon I was moved to another cell. The silence of solitary confinement was frightening. And in the darkness, I did not know if it was day or night. At first, I hoped someone would come and release me. I recalled what Babychan had told me before my arrest, "I will not keep silent. I will try my best to get you out." For days I longed for the police to call out my name.

During the loneliness of this time, I often remembered my wife and children. Feelings of desperation, fear, and doubt swept over me in fierce waves. I could not seem to steady myself before the next onslaught. I could not say one word of praise.

Satan himself seemed to be taunting me, "You will end up inside these four walls...Never again will you see your family...You have been caught in a terrible trap..."

I tried to outpace the thoughts, but they bombarded my mind relentlessly. "You knew what you were doing was risky. Now look at you! See your reward? You were a stupid man. You could have been home with your lovely wife and children...You had a good job. You were blessed, but you weren't satisfied. You wanted to spread the gospel to the Arabs! Now your life is over. Will your labors have accomplished anything? There is no way out..."

Even if I were to miraculously escape the hangman's noose, I would surely be kept in prison for many years, I worried. *What will become of my wife and children? How will I ever find them again?*

Sweat trickled in rivulets down my body. My lips felt parched. I continued pacing the length of my cell, sure that I was going mad. "O Lord," I wept, "the bonds of death have encompassed me."

Suddenly Someone entered the cell. I could see a strange light, and I could hear a musical recitation from Hebrews 12:1: "...we are surrounded by such a great cloud of witnesses, let us throw off everything that hinders and the sin that so easily entangles, and let us run with perseverence the race marked out for us."

The light drove out my fear and replaced it with hope. Immediately I felt consoled. It seemed as if this light filtered itself into and through me, filling me with the power of faith. I became aware of a great multitude of witnesses around me. Into my mind flashed a host of martyrs who had laid down their lives on the altar of faith.

I knew the Light was Jesus. I understood. Moving closer to Him, I began to shout His name. The Holy Spirit filled me afresh, and in the power of the Spirit, I began to praise the Lord. As His glory filled my soul, I could not stop thanking Him and reveling in His presence. Although I was still in solitary confinement and my future was just as uncertain as before, joy rushed through my being. Of all people, I was most blessed. Jesus was with me. And He would never leave me!

The next day, some of the prisoners were told to clean the cells. Those who remained were packed together while their cells were being cleaned. That is how Brother Panicker, Jacob, and I came together. We moved toward one another instinctively and embraced.

Making our way to a corner, we prayed, sharing an immeasurable joy. In our prayers, we commended Brother Solomon and his beloved wife, Leelamma, into the hands of the Lord.

After this all-too-brief interlude, the prisoners were taken to their separate cells. At 11 a.m. the police began to call out our names. Because of their peculiar accent, it was difficult for us to distinguish even our own names. They called John Panicker "Jehangir Pankeer" and Jacob Thomas "Yakkub Thumas." I was "Ghorghi Ghon."

Leelamma was brought from the women's lock-up, and she stood with us. We stared at one another without a word. If we had opened our mouths, we would have burst into tears.

Finally, we were herded into a van that was itself like a prison cell, then chained and driven to another prison in Sharjah.

When we were first brought to this prison, we were put in a cell used for cutting hair. Our food, which consisted of white rice served with a vegetable curry, was placed on a large plate over the heap of hair. We ate it with chained hands, the food sticking on our faces and beards. The food tasted delicious! The scene reminded me of the bearded beggars in India who ate waste food from hotels. I praised God for counting me worthy to suffer for my Lord.

After our meal, we were again escorted to a large van, and handcuffed for the long journey to a prison in Abu Dhabi. Leelamma was with us, but we could not find her husband among the other prisoners.

To Mukthar Prison

Because we had distributed the gospel in seven Arab states in the U.A.E., we learned we had to face each as they prepared their formal charges against us.

Our case report from Sharjah was forwarded to police headquarters in Abu Dhabi. After reading the document, the officials presumed we were notorious gangsters, spies, or foreign agents. In terror of us, they tightened security.

When our names were called, we heard Solomon's name, but he was nowhere to be found. Meanwhile, Leelamma was ordered to go to another location. She looked at us with inexpressible sadness. Fear and cold made her jaw shiver uncontrollably. Since it was winter and bitterly cold, I handed her my coat for protection. Then we were taken to the lock-up at the back of the police station.

The next day, we were transferred to the Mukthar prison. It was a terrible place. The prisoners were little more than human skeletons. Many were close to death.

A hundred and fifty prisoners were crammed into two small rooms and a hall twenty feet by eight feet. Another room served as latrine. We searched for Brother Solomon but could not find him. We did learn, however, that Leelamma was taken to a prison near ours.

We were jammed so close together with the prisoners that we had barely enough space to sit and no place to rest our hands. We deeply grieved over the pitiful condition of the other prisoners. Their bodies smeared with their own fecal matter, they huddled together for warmth.

In the morning, we were fed keema (curry made out of rotten meat) and cuppoose (pita bread). Since we had no plates, the cuppoose was used to receive the keema. First we ate the curry, then the cuppoose. Fortunately, we were able to obtain a plastic bottle, which we cut in half to make two containers to hold our food and drink.

Some days we were served "fish biriyani," fish boiled with the intestines and dirt in a mixture with rice. The taste was bitter and thoroughly unpalatable. The food was served in a large pan so that prisoners had to eat it together. As soon as the food was brought to the cell, everyone would start pushing and shoving. If some of the biriyani fell on the floor, it was eaten nevertheless. I could not! It seemed better to starve.

We huddled there for about two and a half weeks, exhausted and sick with hunger. The sulaimani we received morning and evening sustained our lives.

Twice a day the police would count us. Many times they would count incorrectly and would have to repeat it. The roll call was not always intelligible. If we did not say "nam" (yes) when our names were called, blows would follow.

In all our suffering, we prayed and worshiped the Lord regularly. When others fell asleep, we awoke to pray and sing together. Two or three of the other prisoners came to hear our songs.

Some asked how we reached this prison. When I explained everything, one exclaimed in wonder, "Then you are like the apostles of the early days of Christianity. In you, we find Peter, James, and John!" As we talked, another decided to give his life to Jesus Christ.

He was the first soul that we won for Jesus in that prison. Others—Arabs, Indians, and Pakistanis—soon received Christ as their Savior as well.

As we talked to the other prisoners, we learned of the terrible suffering they endured. The spirits of many were broken by the cruelty of life in the prison.

An Egyptian named Mohammed, for example, had been released and was preparing to return to his native land. Since he had been separated from his wife and children for years, he rejoiced over the thought that in a few hours he would be reunited with them.

Suddenly he was rearrested and returned to this horrible prison! When he questioned why, his captors beat him mercilessly. As a result, Mohammed lost his mind and roamed about the prison narrating the scene of his imaginary reunion with his family. He had been wrongly accused of being a counterfeiter. When the police finally realized their folly, it was too late. He was insane.

A man from Baluchistan, convicted of murder and imprisoned at the age of 28, was still there in his sixties. He had no idea what the world was like. His desire to see the world had long since died. He no longer remembered the faces of his wife and children.

Some in the Mukthar prison had been arrested simply for losing their passports and had been in jail for years as a result. They had many tales of anguish. Their experiences numbed my mind.

It has been said that to be in an Arab jail means "the end of life." We thought that we had surely fallen into such an endless chain of misery and pain and that only our execution would end it for us. With the stench of death hanging about us, we seemed unable to bear the anxiety. We hoped that if our fate were to be death, it would come soon. The expectation was more fierce than death itself.

Longing for Families

Prisoners accused of minor offenses were given short terms. When they were released, we gave them the telephone numbers of our homes and of fellow believers. Our families, however, did not get any information, and of course we knew nothing about them.

We decided to seek help from Al Asaili, Solomon's Arab friend. He reminded me of Jonathan, Saul's son, in the Old Testament. When Saul plotted to kill David, Jonathan saved David. Such a Jonathan was Al Asaili, and we gave his phone number to a prisoner who was released. He promised to contact Al Asaili.

Meanwhile, our wives had no idea whether we were dead or alive or where we were. Finally, we heard from a new prisoner that our families had been under police custody. We were overwhelmed at this news. Where were they? What was their condition? We broke down and wept.

Once again I felt numb and my thoughts wandered back to the past. I saw the lovely faces of my family—all smiling at me. My mind focused on Mary, who was not only my wife but my friend. I remembered clearly the day we met...

In 1979 I went to Bombay on a short vacation. Brother K. M. Samuel, my roommate in Sharjah, had a niece named Mary who worked as a registered nurse in Bombay. He arranged for our proper meeting.

Mary was born and brought up in Itarsi, a town in Central India. I found her to be a modest, born-again Christian woman and eventually asked her to marry me. I told her of my dedication to the Lord's ministry and that I wanted my wife to be a partner with me in ministry.

"Think and pray about this, Mary," I said. "You can give me an answer in two or three days."

She prayed, and her answer came after only two days. She happily decided to share her life with me for the glory of God, and we were united in holy matrimony by Reverend K. V. Abraham on October 6, 1979.

After our wedding, I set out for Dubai. My wife quit her job and joined me on the last day of the year. We lived in the state of Sharjah, though I worked in Dubai. Before long, Mary found employment in the Al Quisimi Hospital in Sharjah, which was run by the British Company. As a registered nurse, she too had an average salary. In due time God gave us two lovely daughters. Until 1983, we lived happily and were involved in the Lord's work...

Reality jerked me back to the present. The news of my family brought by the new prisoner grieved me deeply. With a stabbing pain in my heart, I sat silently in my cell.

CHAPTER 5

Night Visitor

One night while asleep, I felt Someone standing near me. His voice was clear. "In the morning, visitors are coming to see you." I woke up immediately and roused Brother Panicker and Jacob.

"Tomorrow some people are coming to see us," I announced. "The angel of God told me."

Friday was visitors' day, and as always, many came to see their loved ones. The police would call out the names of prisoners, who would then go to the bars to see their visitors. Only a few minutes were allowed. We waited eagerly for our names to be called.

Finally, our turn came. "Ghorghi Ghon, Jehangir Pankeer, Yakkub Thumas!" Jumping to our feet, we brushed through other prisoners to approach the bars. Who would be coming to see us? Because of how we all looked, it was difficult for visitors to tell who was who. We had all grown mustaches and beards, and our emaciated bodies were covered with dirt.

Scanning the area, we suddenly saw Ravi, a native of Kerala whom we had brought to the faith. We stretched out our hands through the bars.

"Ravi! Ravi!" He hurried over to us. We were given so little time to visit. Quickly passing fruit to us through the bars, he spoke of how he had searched for us in many prisons and gave us words of comfort. Then he left.

Since we were not expecting any other visitors, we trudged back to our seats. Although our hearts were heavy, we felt grateful for the love of Christ that had just embraced us.

Some time before when Abubaker, an Arab prisoner, was released, we had asked him to contact Al Asaili. He promised in the name of Allah to do so. Al Asaili and his wife, Amina, loved Solomon and Leelamma like a brother and sister. They used their money and influence to try to save us. It was because of them that on that Friday we were taken to the warden's office, where our wives and my daughter, Sara, were waiting for us.

At first, Mary could not recognize me. I looked exhausted and disfigured with filth. My hair was long and messy, and my mustache was untrimmed.

"Mary!" I called. She looked bewildered.

"Jonichaya!" her cry filled the room. Then she embraced me and wept.

Panicker and his wife also embraced with deep emotion. Seeing these outbursts, even the guards wiped tears from their eyes.

I gazed at Sara, who was staring blankly at me. She had a look of compassion in her eyes but thought I was a stranger. Impulsively she stretched out her hand and gave me a plastic butterfly, then stepped back.

Soon they were gone, and the loneliness crushed our hearts again.

Through a friend named Razak, we eventually learned that Brother Solomon had been released after eighteen days in prison and was now safe in Bombay. For this we praised the Lord!

Arab Newspapers Proclaim the Gospel

We were given considerable notoriety in the public press. In addition to *The Indian Express, Times of India,* and even *Malayala Manorama,* Arab newspapers such as *Khaleej Times, Al-Kalij,* and the *Emirate News* publicized details about our arrest under the heading "Kidnap Case." Thus our situation became widely known.

Those who read Arab newspapers condemned us roundly. In "Letters to the Editor," no one expressed sympathy for us—or at least no such letters were printed. Contributors said we should have our heads cut off, be stoned to death, or be hanged.

Although unknown to us at the time, the Arab newspapers printed entire copies of the Gospels and tracts we had secretly distributed. These tracts contained the message of salvation

EMIRATES NEWS 9-

Court and Police beat

4-member missionary cell held in Sharjah

SHARJAH (EN): Sharjah police has arrested a four-member missionary cell, all Indians for carrying out missionary activities against Islam.

The cell was accused of sending books, messages and leaflets to Muslims residing in the UAE through the addresses and P.O. Box numbers found in the telephone directory.

The members of the group arrested include Jacob Thomas, 41, a mechanic, Lilaman Soloman Matid, a 43-year-old nurse; and G. George John, a 31-year-old airconditioning technician.

The accused told the police that they had links with a missionary group in the US since 1979 and that they got the books and leaflets in Arabic from the US based group.

القبض على «خلية»

TIMES OF INDIA 9-2-83

Indians face jail for conversion bid

BAHRAIN, February 8 (PTI): Five Indians face up to two years in jail for allegedly trying to convert Muslims in the United Arab Emirates (UAE) to Christianity.

Authorities said that four men and one woman had links with a United States missionary society. They allegedly sent books and pamphlets to people in the Emirates asking them to become Christians.

The five are being held in prison in Sharjah, according to reports here.

This collection of news articles from the Arab and Indian press describes the arrests of the Christians.

نفس هالكة فى صباح الدينونة
A LOST SOUL ON JUDGMENT MORNING

PEACE OF MIND
IN A TROUBLED WORLD

طوفان التبشير

Some of the confiscated gospel tracts were published in Arab newspapers, as these torn-out scraps illustrate.

through Jesus Christ. We rejoiced that the newspapers did far more for us in one day than what we had accomplished in four years. This was indeed a miracle! God had used the enemy to proclaim the gospel.

Into the Dungeon

One day we were taken to the Abudhalin police headquarters for interrogation. Leelamma also was brought there from her prison. We sat waiting for a whole day with no idea why we had been brought together like this. By evening we were taken to Shafia prison and locked up with the insane.

The next morning we were taken by van to a police station in Alain, 250 miles away. En route we shared the gospel with the guards. They only heaped abuse on us.

"If Isa Nabi is your Savior," they mocked, "let Him save you now!"

Brother Panicker and I were linked by a chain tied to our wrists. We thought of ourselves as being linked by gospel principles, which form a powerful, unbreakable tie.

Holding up our chains as did our spiritual predecessor Paul, we said, "So then, King Agrippa, I was not disobedient to the vision from heaven" (Acts 26:19).

The van stopped suddenly, shaking us up so that the chains cut into our wrists. We were in front of the Alain police station, which looked like a beautiful mansion surrounded by a well-kept garden. We were ordered to sit outside the office of the Director of Police.

All four of us—Panicker, Jacob, Leelamma, and I—were in a deplorable condition from lack of food, sleep, and sanitation. None of us had been able to bathe since our arrest and we were filthy. Our hair was long and dirty and, in the case of the men, our beards and mustaches were ragged.

Our case reports were presented to the Alain authorities, and we were again handed over to the police. Thinking of what might befall us next, we felt anxious.

Soon more policemen arrived. After removing our chains, they ordered Jacob and me to carry a heavy safe to the second floor of the building. In the presence of armed guards, we tried to lift the safe but couldn't. Another laborer was provided and with much difficulty we lifted it to the first floor. Having gone many days without food, we were totally exhausted and close to fainting. But somehow we kept struggling and managed to get it up to the second floor.

By the time we returned to where Brother Panicker was waiting, Leelamma had been taken to the women's prison. We prayed for her safety. Soon we were escorted to an underground prison, about twenty-five feet below ground.

The cell was cold and so dark that it was impossible to tell day from night. Only a little air entered the room. We had no idea how long we were to spend in that place.

Time passed slowly and painfully. We were given one blanket each to spread on the ground and use as a cover. We decided to use one to spread on the floor, another as a pillow, and the third to cover all our bodies. In spite of the crudity of our arrangements, sleep at night was almost pleasant, certainly welcome.

We prayed often, and other prisoners would sometimes listen.

As usual, we were not alone in the dungeon. Among the prisoners was a man from Egypt who had been falsely accused of a crime. Another had sold his birthright and gone after riches. Some of the prisoners were Indians. On the wall one had written, "Indian Embassy Moordabad." This indicated that the Indian embassies in other lands would do nothing to help its citizens. As a result, national feeling was alien to these prisoners.

As for us, our wives appealed to the Indian Embassy, but not one finger was moved to help us. We were expendable. We believed that countries like Britain or America would never allow one of their citizens to remain in an Arab prison for wrongdoing; they would surely look into the matter.

Tortures in the Sharjah Prison

One day while I was drinking sulaimani, a police-man ordered me to clean the paths to the head-quarters. My weakened state made this chore next to impossible. I fainted. Once I was revived, however, I had to continue my work.

Arabs spit from wherever they sit, and I had to remove the spittle with bare hands. In my semi-conscious state, it seemed more than I could do. But the face of my Lord as the Roman soldiers spat on Him appeared in my mind. With that image in focus, I managed to do as ordered.

Afterwards, the police transported me to another place in a jeep. There I was ordered to load a lorry (truck) of thabuk, a large brick. "O Lord, help me!" I agonized. Sensing the pres-ence of an angel to strengthen me, I was able to complete the work.

Back in my cell, I found that lunch had already been served. Without any food, I lay in a corner and slept. When I awoke, it was morning. My strength was virtually gone.

Food in this place was brought from the police canteen, usually by a man from Kerala. Discovering that he was a kind man, I gave him the telephone number of my wife's uncle Abra-ham, who lived somewhere in Alain. I begged him to tell Abraham that we were in this prison. To his credit, he did.

But considering the special nature of our crime, we were not allowed to have visitors. Abraham and my aunt were denied permission to enter. However, a police officer who had formerly been on duty where my aunt worked happened to see her, and with his help she entered.

She burst into tears as soon as she saw us. The parcel she brought was thrust unceremoniously through the bars. It contained thirty chapates (a kind of bread), eggs, and meat. Hungrily we divided the food equally among us and ate.

It was the plan of our captors to move us frequently so no one would know where we were. We were taken to the Al-Alain prison, then transported back to the Alain prison. Who could possibly keep our families informed?

But Abraham was faithful. He kept up with us and telephoned our wives. As soon as the message reached them, they came to see us with our children. We experienced joy in our reunions, but also great sorrow because no one knew when death might come.

After seven days in this prison, we were marched to an office where we faced a huge man with a booming voice. This Mulla, one of the highest religious authorities in the country, could not understand any language but Arabic.

In his presence stood three missionary doctors from the hospital in Alain who had been summoned in connection with our case. They smiled lovingly at us, and so we tried to speak to them in English. Immediately, the Mulla shouted at us and ordered the police to remove the missionaries. Thinking he meant us, the police jerked us from the room. This mistake infuriated the giant and embarrassed the police. Thoroughly confused, they stood staring and immobilized.

Livid by now, the Mulla screamed, "Khullum Bara!" (Pull them all out!)

The police snapped to life and dragged us back down to the underground cell below street level.

Here we met a Muslim youth from Kerala who was imprisoned because he did not possess a proper visa. Hearing us pray for the Arabs, who he knew were our enemy, he wondered at our religion.

"Jesus taught us to love our enemies and pray for those who abuse us," we explained. At once his soul caught a glimpse of the love of Christ, and he accepted Jesus as his Savior.

The next morning we were taken to the police headquarters in Abu Dhabi, where all the reports had been sent. Thus all the investigations from the seven states of U.A.E. were now over. The case would then be tried and judged at the religious court of Sharjah, where we were officially arrested.

Since no van was ready to return us to Sharjah police headquarters, we were forced to do manual labor while we waited. We carried heavy loads of brick and other supplies used for construction about a tenth of a mile away. The work was exhausting, and when we were finally allowed to sleep, it was without any food.

The next day we were taken on a three-hour journey to the Sharjah out-prison, an iron-fenced fortress containing some five hundred prisoners.

Again the stench from the open latrines assaulted us, and we observed the effects of many cruel tortures among the other prisoners. One pathetic man had had all his fingernails and toenails pulled out because he had been smuggling hashish and caras. *It would have been kinder to shoot him*, I thought. *Such cruel tortures!*

At our assigned cell there was no room to sit, and the other prisoners refused to let us in. They grabbed us around the neck and pushed us out. Finally, we were allowed to sit in a corridor.

Eventually the warden became our friend, and we began to feel that the worst was over. He allowed us to have visitors any time. This new freedom delighted my wife, who came immediately with a friend. They began to feed us fruit as if we were children. Later, Mary returned with Brother Panicker's wife and our children. We were able to visit together in the warden's office and were all greatly comforted.

In this out-prison, the other inmates began to turn their attention to us. They were fascinated by our behavior and our compassion for them. They told us their own sad stories, and we tried to comfort them. Many came to us for counseling and some for prayer. Amid the suffering in the cell, we turned into ministers of the Lord, and this prison became our church.

Where once we had suffered great cruelty, we were now loved and even esteemed. People from different Arab states began coming to see us. Many shed tears over our plight. Angry public opinion melted away as many people started praying for us.

Some of our fellow-believers in Sharjah who had kept us in prayer broke down in tears at the iron fence, and we wept too. The words of Jesus were very real, "I was in prison and you came to visit me" (Matthew 25:36). Leelamma, we learned, was released on bail with the help of Al Asaili about the time we arrived at the out-prison.

A prison worker by the name of Shumughadar, who enjoyed the authority and liberty of a warden, had once been a member of a Panchayatt (part of the government). Because he seemed to possess special skills to cajole the authorities, Shumughadar soon gained the affection of the police officials.

Seeing our sad plight, he took us to a clean and spacious storeroom and let us stay there.

Few policemen were able to get visas, passports, or tickets because they refused to learn and were basically lazy. Most could not count to ten! Wealth from the oil fields made learning unnecessary. Sometimes an Arab would spend money for another and compel him to learn, but this was the exception.

A story was told about an Arab in the air force whom an English pilot was teaching to fly. When the Arab found it difficult, he said to the Englishman, "Why should I learn all these things? If war breaks out, you will fly; I will pay." This is the attitude of the average Arab.

As a result of his communication abilities, Shumughadar handled both prisoners and jailers with dexterity. He liked his job so much that even after the terms of his imprisonment were up, he remained. Here he was free. Some prisoners who did not have passports were sent by boat to India or Pakistan. Some were exiled every month, and Shumughadar made money gathering their plane tickets and selling them!

From the storeroom, our benefactor provided us with clean blankets and prepared a place for us to sleep. Providing us with cheese and bread and coffee, he seemed to us an angel sent from God.

In the middle of the night, he would bring water for us to bathe, and for several days we had fresh baths and good sleep.

One morning we were unable to get breakfast. When Shumughadar found out, he provided us with jam, cheese, cuppoose, and Nescafe—unheard-of luxuries.

One day he overheard us talking to another prisoner about Jesus Christ and said he wanted to know about the peace we had in our hearts. We talked to him for a long time. That night he accepted our Savior and found the peace he needed. We learned that he had been forsaken by his wife, rejected by family and friends, and had suffered a lot in his tragic life. He began to pray with a contrite heart.

Soon we taught him the first few lines of a beautiful Malayalam chorus, which he recorded on tape and learned to sing. He became our go-between with the police, who in turn became our friends.

Many people came to see us, bringing food, encouragement, and much love.

CHAPTER 6

Released

Where are they? Are you still keeping them in this country?" the Mulla's voice boomed over the telephone.

"Who?" the Sharjah out-prison official returned fearfully.

"Ghorghi Ghon, Jehangir Pankeer, Yakkub Thumas!"

"Yes, they are still here..."

"Do not keep them there for a single minute longer!" the Mulla barked.

The official trembled at the voice of the Mulla. Astonished, the prison authorities had to be certain they were hearing him correctly. "Release them! They are to be sent out of our country immediately!" the Mulla shouted.

God had heard our prayers and delivered us. We who had expected to die were suddenly set free. But it took a while for us to find this out.

Accused of a crime punishable by death, we were awaiting our day in court with much concern. At the court in Sharjah, we would have no right to a defense because that would be considered a defamation of the court. To argue against a charge is another crime, and the consequence would be double punishment. Complicating matters further, the Mulla was the judge, and his sentences were always carried out. The injustice of this court reminded me of ancient Rome. The fate of a captive was determined by the way the emperor held his thumb!

Al Asaili, however, succeeded in getting us released by paying a fee to an influential official in the U.A.E.

The police came quickly, pushing and shoving us from our cell with such roughness that we were sure this was our death call. We were chained, herded into a van, and—much to our surprise—driven at high speed to the Dubai Airport. At the airport, I was taken to my old office, still in chains. The airport manager and the administrator were astonished to see me, especially in my condition.

Uncertain whether they recognized me, I blurted, "I'm George John."

Suddenly I was surrounded by my co-workers, who showed me much affection. Even my guards changed their attitude toward me when they saw this. Only then did I realize that we were going to be released. I had been brought to the airport to close out my employment records.

Meanwhile, Brother Panicker, who had been an official in the Dubasi Transpish Company, was taken to his office, where his account and records were quickly closed. His supervisor, however, treated him with contempt.

Brother Jacob was taken to his old office in Sharjah, where the same business was transacted.

While waiting for Jacob, I had a chance to speak to the policemen guarding me. Their eyes filled with tears as they simply said, "Isa Allah-hi." (Jesus is God.)

It is customary for an Arab prisoner to have palm and fingerprints made and photographs taken. Before returning to the Sharjah out-prison, we were taken to another police station to have this done. They made fourteen palm prints of me, and too many photos.

The police allowed me to telephone Mary to tell her about my release. The news spread quickly. It seemed that within just minutes visitors began to gather at the out-prison. The police and Arab prisoners were fascinated by the great love being poured out to us by Christians, regardless of denomination and language.

Our joy over being released was tempered, however, with the knowledge that it was easy for an Arab to change his mind. It would take a few days to finalize our release and deport us to India, and we could not relax until we actually set foot on Indian soil.

Meanwhile, we worked to get our families out of the country before us, fearing harm could come to them while we waited. Some believers collected money, bought their tickets, and helped them get ready for their return to Bombay.

Our families visited us just before they flew home. We were still in our ugly prison uniforms when we said goodbye, expressing our eager hope to join them before long.

Finally our day came. Thousands of well-wishers greeted us at the Dubai Airport when we arrived. The police had a hard time maintaining control as everyone wanted to touch and kiss us, many of them weeping.

"We will meet again in the mid-air. Maranatha!" The cry rang out. Many shouted, "Hallelujah!"

At eleven p.m. on the sixteenth of March 1983, our chains were removed. Even the police performing this function beamed as they handed over our passports, tickets, and the balance of our salaries from our old jobs.

Six long weeks after our arrest, we were in the air on our way home and to freedom.

At the airport in Bombay, another crowd awaited us. Thousands of them, coming forward to give their lives to the Lord Jesus Christ. This was the harvest of our suffering.

Many who saw Mary and I embrace wept with tears of joy. Our hearts filled with gratitude to our Lord that we were counted worthy to suffer for His name's sake.

George John, Mary, and their children continue to witness for the Lord Jesus Christ.

CHAPTER 7

Risking All for Christ

Despite the fierce opposition to Christianity in Arab lands, many others like ourselves continue to risk their lives for the sake of the gospel. Brother Nelson, a devout Indian Christian in Qatar, is a dynamic example.

The small peninsula of Qatar juts into the Persian Gulf like a missile pointed northward at Tehran and the Caspian Sea. An independent Arab nation with a half-million citizens, Qatar boasts a per capita Gross National Product of $11,600, exceeded only by the United Arab Emirates and Kuwait individually and equal to the combined output of Israel, Jordan, Lebanon, and Egypt.

With modest oil reserves compared to its neighbors, Qatar nevertheless is heavily populated by foreign workers. Many workers are from India, which looks on Arab countries as Mexicans view the U.S.—a source of work and wealth.

Although Qatar is strict about its Muslim religion, it does permit the building of churches. Believers, however, are not allowed to prosely-

tize or preach beyond the church confines.
Local citizens, presumed to be Muslims even if
they convert, are forbidden to enter a church.
Since many have Christian friends and are inter-
ested in knowing more about Christ, they visit in
their homes, which is permissible.

Brother Nelson, an employee in the government water department in the city of Doha, had
been holding meetings whenever possible in his
house and in the Apostolic Church he attended.
On one occasion, he was chatting earnestly with
a Hindu friend on his veranda. Although he was
on private property, someone overheard him
mention the name of Christ and complained to
the police. Soon a car drove up and he was
hauled off to the police station.

As Brother Nelson was being booked, a sheik
standing nearby overheard the charges and in-
tervened. "I will take full responsibility for the
prisoner," he informed the authorities. "If I am
not able to do what I want to do, I'll bring him
back to you." The sheik's tone seemed ominous
and the police released Brother Nelson.

In Arab countries, a sheik carries considerable authority because he owns property and
often holds high office in government. Dressed
in Western shoes and a long, white robe and
turban with a black rope, the sheik hurried
Brother Nelson out of the police station and to
his car. Nelson felt frightened. Where was the
sheik taking him? To prison where he would

endure severe punishment, or worse? Finally, the car pulled up in front of a house. The sheik ushered him inside to the living room and faced him.

"I was listening to all that happened at the police station—the complaints, everything. What I want to know is, are you a believer in Christ, and how serious are you?" The sheik's dark eyes penetrated Brother Nelson.

Nelson took a deep breath and decided to tell the truth. "I'm a witness for the Lord, sharing the gospel of Jesus Christ."

The sheik raised his hand abruptly. "Wait a minute, wait a minute! I have a problem for you." He stepped backward and motioned for Brother Nelson to sit. "An aunt of mine is bedridden and has been for some time. You pray to your God for her. If she is cured, I'll accept your God as the greatest."

Thinking carefully about his response, Brother Nelson asked, "Have you prayed to your god?"

"Yes, of course. I have been praying many days…"

"Has anything happened? Has your aunt's condition improved?" Nelson pressed.

"No, nothing has happened, so I'm giving you the opportunity to prove that your God is superior to mine."

Brother Nelson accepted the challenge. With heartfelt sincerity and earnestness, he bowed and prayed.

"Lord, Your name is being put to the test, so you have to prove Yourself. Please, Lord, cure this aunt because he is prepared to accept you as the true God. Here is a convert ready for You to take over. I believe You will hear my prayer. Exonerate me also from any complaint this man is going to lay against me. And please strengthen my faith..."

He kept praying, not knowing when to stop because he felt a great burden for the sheik and his aunt. Some time later, Brother Nelson heard the noise of cups and saucers being shaken together, and opened his eyes furtively to see what was happening.

Before him stood the aunt offering him a cup of tea. She had risen from her cot, gone to the kitchen, prepared tea, and brought it to him.

The sheik stood beside her smiling. "Do you believe in my God?" Brother Nelson asked.

"Yes," the sheik said simply. "I believe and accept your God as the greatest. But don't go around telling everyone I have accepted. I give you the assurance that I believe in God. Meanwhile, I will come to your meetings. I will visit you, and you must pray for me. Please come and pray for my family and my problems."

The sheik kept his promise and came to Brother Nelson's meetings. Nelson still holds

Bible studies in his house and gives messages to any group of Christians who invite him to speak.

Secret Groups

Saudi Arabia occupies the largest portion of the Arabian Peninsula. As in the other Arab nations of the region, Christians are secretly spreading the gospel at great personal risk.

Among them is M. C. George, who began his ministry in Saudi Arabia while on a tourist visa. As a tourist he visited approximately eighty homes and started several prayer groups. Every Friday and Sunday evening, he met with groups in different houses in various areas of the country. When the time came for him to return to his home, he left Saudi Arabia with great reluctance—a modern Macedonian cry ringing in his ears: *Come back and help us! We need guides and leaders in the study of God's Word. We're sheep without a shepherd.*

Back home, he and his wife fasted and prayed for employment in Saudi Arabia so he could continue his gospel work. Eventually receiving an employment visa to work for a construction company, Brother George returned, rejoicing that the Lord had answered their prayers.

Sixth in line on his job, he soon found himself out of work and had to search again. But like the apostle Paul, he used each job transfer as an opportunity to start another prayer group. In the nine years he spent in Saudi, Brother George formed eight groups. Between 300 and 350 new converts attended the secret meetings.

One day the Hindu driver of a Christian friend, located 150 miles away in Alkobar, decided he wanted to attend a meeting and set off in his lorry for Dhamam. After his arrival, he spoke with several Arab drivers, one of whom asked if he had friends locally. The Hindu driver said yes and gave him the address.

Later, as he and Brother George were praying in his home, the police arrived with the Arab driver and caught them in prayer. They were taken to the police station for questioning.

In some countries the police can search a house for any cause. But in the Gulf countries authorities usually don't search unless they have obtained permission from the government. Consequently, Christian believers who smuggle literature to Arab nations quickly hide it after their arrival. It's not considered wise to leave the material in full view—just in case. So the policeman was not looking for literature. But he did catch Brother George and the Hindu driver kneeling with clasped hands, Christian-style.

While waiting for the inspector at the police station, they took advantage of the situation and prayed openly in the middle of the room.

Finally the inspector arrived. "Who is your sponsor?" he asked Brother George.

When George replied, the inspector said, "But your sponsor is 150 miles away from here. What business have you in Dhamam?"

Brother George talked with the officer for a few moments. Finally satisfied with his answer, the inspector said, "I'll call your sponsor and ask him to come immediately and get his driver."

The sponsor paid his driver's fine and they were released. Again God worked a miracle on behalf of His faithful witnesses.

The Secret Good Samaritan

While M. C. George was walking to the post office one sweltering summer day, he fainted on the road, cutting his forehead on a broken six-inch pipe. For two hours he lay in the drainage ditch beside the road.

As in the story of the Good Samaritan, many people came by and, thinking he was dead, went on their way. No one—not even the police—offered to help him. Finally a worker from a prince's family who was driving alone stopped. Discovering that Brother George was still alive though unconscious, the stranger lifted him into the front seat of his car and drove him to the hospital.

There a doctor ordered X-rays and stitched up his wounds. When he came to, the X-ray technician explained to Brother George where he was and how he got there.

"Someone from the prince's family brought you here," he explained. "Otherwise no one could touch you because you had been injured. Of course, no one knew whether you were dead. If you had died, the man from the prince's family would take the case." This modern Good Samaritan had offered to pay the bill if the patient had no money.

"What is the name of this man?" Brother George asked the doctor. "I want to thank him."

The stranger's name, George learned, was Mr. Belack. He worked in a business for an Arab prince. His wife also worked in the city. Belack too was a Christian who actively shared the gospel.

Where he worked, Brother Belack found many opportunities to share the gospel. In charge of a store, he witnessed directly, using Arabic Bibles supplied to him by The Voice of the Martyrs. Since he stocked all kinds of merchandise in his small store, he was able to keep the Bibles well hidden among his stock.

"Wise as a serpent and harmless as a dove," he would lay an open Bible on the counter whenever he saw someone coming. Frequently the customer would look at the book so casually displayed and ask what it was.

"I tell them it is a good story to read and give them a Bible," he explained to Brother George with a smile. "Since I can read no Arabic myself, this is my best method for distributing the Word of God."

Although Arab Muslims listened to what he had to say about Jesus, Pakistani Muslims were dead set against him.

One day Brother Belack boldly left a Bible open as he distributed other Bibles to different shops. Though it was dangerous to do this, the Lord protected his efforts. He also distributed Arabic tracts that he received from the pastor of the Arab-Christian church. Somehow, over a period of nine years he never had any problems, and this made him a valuable aide to The Voice of the Martyrs.

The "Good Samaritan" who worked for the prince turned out to be a Christian. It was not in his code of behavior to leave a wounded—or dead—man lying on the street.

Or is there a hidden bond that draws Christians to one another? The bond of one body, one Spirit, one hope, one faith—the bond of peace that is unique.

Strong in Faith

"God chose the foolish things of the world to shame the wise; God chose the weak things of the world to shame the strong" (1 Corinthians 1:27).

Thomas Matthew was strong in faith when he worked in the office of an oil company in Saudi. Some called him a fanatic, even crazy.

And he was—crazy about Jesus. God, always short of good raw material, was able to use him remarkably.

Brother Matthew distributed Christian literature to everyone he could persuade to accept it. He received much of the material from a few American Christians who worked with him. The literature was in Arabic, not in his native language.

Inside the oil company compound, an international enclave beyond the reach of normal police interference, Brother Matthew handed out literature with great enthusiasm to Arab workers. But since the books were about Jesus Christ, some Arabs threatened to notify the police.

Undaunted, he said, "Jesus told me to do this."

Since there were Arab Christians and a chapel inside the compound, no one could stop him, and he continued with his personal mission for two or three years. Arabs, of course, could carry the literature beyond the limits of the compound, though at their own risk. Sometimes Matthew even put reading material in Arab cars that entered the confines.

Eventually he began mailing literature to addresses that he selected from the phone book. In this way he sent many thousands of pieces by mail. Although the authorities received complaints, Matthew was so discrete that no one could identify the culprit.

Brother Matthew was ecstatic when he learned that his efforts brought someone to Christ. In Hofuf—which according to legend was visited by the apostle Paul—a royal prince and his family accepted Christ as a result of Matthew and other believers. Undoubtedly breached by the mailman, the walls of his grand estate—guarded by two or three watchmen at the gates—could not keep out the gospel.

The prince has many wives with all of their attendant servants. It is not known how many are secretly worshiping. But angels can enter even the most formidable fortresses. Surely God has chosen the weak to confound the mighty.

In Medina there is a large mosque in which meetings are held on Friday. Emboldened by his previous stratagems and on fire for the Lord as ever, Brother Matthew decided to pass out literature to the Muslims. At first they thought he was crazy, though harmless.

Finally, realizing Matthew was crazy about Jesus Christ, the authorities arrested him. Thrown into prison, he was beaten and transferred from place to place so no one would know where he was.

His brother, also a Christian, was communications minister for another country. The ambassador and the foreign affairs minister, a Muslim, were also from his home state. Through the persuasive efforts of directors from The Voice of the Martyrs, these three interceded with the Saudi Arabian ambassador on Matthew's behalf. Matthew was released. But unable to endure the torment, he emerged from prison a mentally broken man.

Meanwhile, prayer groups from many denominations were interceding with God on Matthew's behalf. Eventually, the Saudi government give him not only his freedom, but his pension and wages owed him.

Brother Matthew's zeal for the Lord brought forth much fruit for the kingdom of God. How much, only eternity will tell.

There are many ordinary Christians like myself who use the opportunity to witness for Christ among people deprived of the gospel in a predominantly Islamic culture. You too can be a light in the darkness.

God is looking for ordinary people who have open hearts and a vision for reaching the lost— wherever they are. Jesus says, "Go into all the world and preach the good news to all creation" (Mark 16:15). This Great Commission was not given only to His first disciples. It is our glorious responsibility and privilege as well.

Jesus cautions, "Do you not say, 'Four months more and then the harvest'? I tell you, open your eyes and look at the fields! They are ripe for harvest" (John 4:35). In these pages you have viewed the ripened fields. You have read gripping, real-people stories of dedicated believers risking all to reap Muslims for Christ. With the inexorable advance of prophesied cataclysmic events in the Middle East, we have little time left to reach these people for our Lord.

I encourage you to pray for the faithful gospel witnesses you have met in this book—and for the many others who still labor for our Savior in these very difficult lands. Make a total, irrevocable commitment of your life to Christ, and determine to follow Him wherever He leads you.

Jesus chose common, ordinary working people who were obedient to Him and filled with His Holy Spirit to fulfill His Great Commission. With these qualities, you too can help reach your world for Christ. You may not be called to the barren sands of the Arabian Peninsula. But God can use you to spread His Word to the Muslim world through your prayers and financial support. And you can begin sharing Christ as a way of life in your own neighborhood, office, or factory.

There are now more Muslim missionaries in the world than Christian missionaries. Who will help turn the tide? Pray that the Lord will open the eyes of more Western Christians to the opportunities among them. And as you pray, ask Him to develop within you His eyes, His mind, His heart.

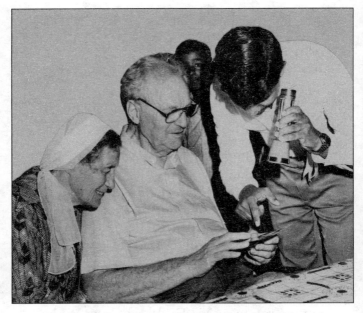

George John explains the photographs and details of his work among the Muslims to Reverend Richard and Sabina Wurmbrand, founders of The Voice of the Martyrs.

For current information on the
Persecuted Church contact:

The Voice of the Martyrs, Inc.
PO Box 443
Bartlesville, OK 74005
(918) 337-8015